The 7 Sins of Being a Mother

The 7 Sins of Being a Mother

Tahira Kashyap Khurrana

❀ juggernaut

JUGGERNAUT BOOKS
C-I-128, First Floor, Sangam Vihar, Near Holi Chowk,
New Delhi 110080, India

First published by Juggernaut Books 2021

10 9 8 7 6 5 4 3 2 1

P-ISBN: 9789391165451
E-ISBN: 9789391165918

Typeset in Adobe Caslon Pro by R. Ajith Kumar, Noida

Printed at Thomson Press India Ltd

To my love for women of all shapes/sizes/moods/ structures/feelings, pre-/post-/none menopausal, with oestrogen/progesterone/testosterone/none, with gravity-defying breasts/silicones/one/none, with children/without. I dedicate this book to women and those who identify as one.

I am a sinner

Contents

Introduction: The Sinning Starts at Forty Weeks

Pregnancy

I was proving to be the worst mother out of her patients. I didn't seem to be into my kid, childbirth hadn't turned me into a being of soft, maternal generosity.

We were in the middle of it, my boy and me. It was a starry night, we were in a plush hotel room, our clothes had left trails on the floor. I was slightly tipsy with the wine I had had at dinner. The protein shake had worked its magic on him. Those were the carefree, guilt-free days of early marriage.

Suddenly I heard my boy say, 'Shabash, shabash,' and then letting out a sigh of satisfaction. I had expected a more horny 'yea baby'. This was like getting encouragement from a PT coach.

I put aside his confidence-boosting words but what I couldn't ignore were the consequences of it – our first unplanned pregnancy. Why do I say first? Because the second, about which I have written in my earlier book, was unplanned too.

How did we manage such a feat twice? Well, we weren't just riding high on hormones, we were also following PT instructions. As soon as we got married, my in-laws began telling us that it took years and years to produce a baby; only if we started now would we manage to have one in three to four years.

My competitive spirit got the better of me, and I produced two in three years. After the 'shabash' night we got cold feet and were very careful and disciplined about contraception. Then we had another blip, but since this was just a blind shot and it usually takes months and years of blind shots to make a baby, we got lazy about taking any precautions. I forgot that my boy had won a teddy bear in archery at a school fest. Always the bullseye!

But let's not digress. This book is about what happens after the pregnancies, about the long, winding road of motherhood. About the comedies, the tragedies, the learnings, the failings and, always, the guilt. When it comes to motherhood, I feel I have been the eternal sinner. Many of these dramas began even before the baby came out.

My first pregnancy came with a huge list of instructions from Mummy, my mother-in-law. One was that I was not to sleep with my boy. She meant sex. This being my first, I tried to follow all the instructions, but my libido was at an all-time high. I don't think I let my boy have a minute of rest, and he wasn't complaining. But the guilt of indulging in carnal pleasures while pregnant was getting to me.

I was expected to have pure, pious thoughts and was even forwarded a few satsangs and discourses along with meditation methods. But inside I felt like Bindu and Helen, the yesteryear vamps who oozed sex appeal. My sin was that not only was I horny but also felt very sexy, despite a baby growing inside me.

I blamed Chandigarh's weather and the good home food for being so aphrodisiacal. But when one post-sex morning my boy reminded me that this was peak summer and I had eaten khichdi the night before, I realized it was all me.

This disconnect of reality versus expectation began to get to me. So we decided to meet a gynaecologist. The doctor asked us, 'Do you have relations?' 'Of course we do! I mean, we are married,' I responded, baffled. She looked at me, rolling her eyes, and repeated herself. 'I know you both are married, but do you have relations with him?'

What the hell was wrong with her? I was about to get up and leave, when my boy squeezed my hand and whispered, 'Sex.' I looked at him even more confused. 'Now, baby?' He frowned and said, 'Idiot, she is talking about us having sex.'

As I look back on the incident, I remember a more recent one where my son came to me saying that his friend had hit the MP. I was very impressed by this eight-year-old's bravery. He had actually done what so many of us dream of. He had struck a member of Parliament!

'Why are you smiling? He hit the main point,' my son said to me, tugging at my kurta. I still couldn't fathom what he was talking about. Switchboard, socket? Then my son gestured to his pelvis. What? Whatever happened to the words 'penis' and 'vagina'!

I should have corrected the gynae back when she used the word 'relations'. Perhaps these cryptic abbreviations wouldn't have trickled down to the next generation. As much as I disliked my doctor and her way of explaining sex to us, she did finally give me the answer I needed.

Yes, it was safe to have 'relations'. 'Biologically and physiologically, you are allowed.' As we were about to leave, she added a postscript, 'But religiously speaking, beta, pure thoughts always help.'

As soon as I left her office, my phone beeped. It

was a message from the doctor recommending a book: *Spiritual Thoughts During Pregnancy*. Urgh. I chose to ignore her sermons. Nor did I stop for most of the pregnancy! When it became impossible to do missionary because of my ever-expanding tabletop, we moved to cutlery and spooned instead!

In the meantime, my bump grew and grew. Every few weeks I would look in the mirror and say to myself, 'This is it. I really can't get any bigger than this.' Then I would surprise myself and break my record. My masi would keep asking me if I had become so big that I was getting stuck in doorways. If I wasn't then I had more capacity.

In the final weeks, she flew down to Chandigarh to be a part of my new beginnings. As soon as she arrived, she gave me a big hug and said approvingly, 'Ae honda ae size (this is what they should look like).'

No, she wasn't talking about my bump, but my boobs. Some things never change! I have to admit I was loving it too, though by this point, at nearly nine months, I wasn't feeling sexy any more. From Helen and Bindu I had graduated into becoming a whale, rude noises erupting from deep within my depths every now and then.

I just wanted the baby out. And so my masi, who was always looking for a rescue mission (she could give all the Batmans and James Bonds a real run for their money), decided to launch Operation Labour. You should start having a lot of sex, she told me loudly over lunch. As much as I appreciated her forthrightness, I really didn't think she had to be this explicit while I was with my parents at the dining table.

My father choked on his food, my mother tried to shut Masi up by passing all the food to her, even as my nani nodded her head in agreement. As much as I would have loved to take this advice, I needed to have my partner around. He was in Delhi shooting his first film, feeling young and fresh, while I was struggling with a helium-balloon version of myself and the Masi-and-Nani team.

I whispered to her, 'Masi, he isn't here,' to which she said, 'Taan ki hoya (so what)?' My father could take it no more. He stopped eating and got up to leave. My nani started scolding my mother for not putting enough salt in the food and forcing my poor father to abandon his meal. 'This is what happens if you serve pickle bought from the market,' she said to herself sadly.

Masi realized that sex wasn't a viable option for me,

and so came the next nuskha – moving the nipples. How the f*ck does one move one's nipples? As kids we had practised eyebrow raising, winking, rolling the tongue while sticking it out, heck, even moving the ears, but moving the nipples? How do you train those muscles, ligaments, tissues – whatever makes those nipples?

Masi corrected me saying, 'I mean rub them.' I didn't want to rub any creams over my swollen breasts. Earnestly she said she could do it for me. What? No way was that happening! Later I learnt that nipple stimulation increases oxytocin production, which causes the uterus to contract. I am sure she didn't know any of this, and I wasn't telling her in case she decided to pounce on my nipples.

Her next tip was to have castor oil, taking it either through the nose or mouth. No, I said firmly. After much coaxing I agreed, but on the condition that she would do the sample test first. I didn't let her argument of 'I don't have anything to push out except kidney stones' convince me. I got the better of Masi on that occasion, but she didn't concede defeat. After all, no one leaves a pregnant woman alone, and certainly not Chotu Masi.

She didn't trouble me for the next few days, but couldn't stop herself thereafter. She came to me carrying a whole bunch of needles. She was going to do some acupuncture on me. I asked her, worried, if she had ever done this before. She told me she had researched on Google for the past few days and might just be able to pull it off. You can imagine what my response was. NO.

Her next idea was to make my meals extra hot, that is, loaded with chilli. She believed the spice would help in inducing contractions. Those meals left not just my tongue but also my heart and stomach burning.

December winter in Chandigarh can be painful. You hold in your pee and go only when it is urgent. And here I was, sitting on the ice-cold pot for hours, running chilled water from the jet spray up my frozen butt.

The next day, exhausted, I left for my daily walk (more of a waddle now since I had gained twenty-two kilos!). It didn't take long for Masi to catch up. She apologized for frightening me and gave me another tip. I was to imagine my labour. It's called visualization, she said, beaming.

Okay, this didn't sound so bad. I started visualizing that I was being taken to the hospital with beautiful, blow-dried hair. The doctor asked me to push twice and on the third push the baby came out gently, all smiling and dimpled. The doctor handed it over to me. I caressed the baby's soft skin and it gurgled at me.

Masi was not pleased to see my tranquil, happy face (this was surely not a good sign!) and was about to hit me with another hare-brained idea. I had had enough and sped up so I could be on my own. Her presence was giving me palpitations.

My palpitations didn't stop even after I reached home. My stomach too had started cramping. Maybe the fast walk had been a bit too strenuous. I sat down, closed my eyes and took a few deep breaths. When I opened my eyes I saw Chotu Masi staring at me.

She was smiling triumphantly. 'You are in labour!' What? Seriously? Yay! Excited, we took out the hospital bag we had prepared earlier and waited for the contractions to quicken. On a side note, no amount of nuskhas and tricks helped; all that was required was Chotu Masi's presence!

It was night by the time my contractions became more frequent, coming now every three minutes. My parents who had dozed off in exhaustion were shaken awake by superhero Masi who shouted, 'The girl is going to deliver here only. Get up. Let's go!'

My boy was in the middle of his shoot and could only come the next morning. As we headed to the hospital, I began to use my visualization skills. I convinced myself that labour was going to be as easy as I had imagined – the only thing that would be different was that I hadn't managed the blow-dried hair. As soon as we reached the hospital, I peed myself. I was mortified until the nurses told me that it wasn't pee. My water had burst.

Then I went into active, excruciating, back-breaking labour for the next twelve hours. Night turned into day and day into evening. I went from screaming 'oh shit' to 'crap' to 'f*ck' to finally 'bh*****d'. I was out of my mind.

When my mother-in-law dropped in, I said, 'Behenji ko bula do, Mummy,' referring to the nurse. As soon as she was out of the room, the swearing renewed. Finally I was taken to a birthing chair. As I lay sprawled there, legs spread wide apart, the baby's head nearly emerging, my nani popped into the room, gave me an encouraging smile and told me, 'Just do it!' I really didn't need any Nike slogans thrown at me by my insane family as I moaned and writhed in pain. Terrified that Chotu Masi would join Nani in giving me a pep talk as I was having my 'crowning' moment, I told the doctors not to allow any of my family members into the room.

But my doctor was too distracted by a crisis to pay attention to this. It turned out that my heart rate was dipping and so was the baby's. We went for an emergency caesarean. It was so sudden that they didn't even put a curtain in front of me while operating.

I remember asking stupid questions like, 'Doctor, will I ever be able to pee again?' 'Will I ever be able to have sex again?' The doctor didn't bother responding, and soon I heard the soft wails of a baby.

'It's a boy,' the doctor said with a smile. After a quick clean-up she tried to place the baby in my arms, but I refused. Surprisingly, all the warmth and love that I thought I would feel for the baby just wasn't there.

I simply felt dazed and tired, relieved that it was all over. I was amazed to see the tiny creature who had been growing inside me, who had come out of this crazy journey unscathed. And that's it.

The gynaecologist gave me a judging look and, slightly ashamed by my feelings, or the lack of them, I rubbed my nose against my baby. That's all I could manage. The doctor gave up on me and finally took the baby to the family members waiting outside.

Stitched and cleaned up, I was rolled into my room where he was waiting for me along with a row of happy faces, including my boy who had arrived halfway through the whole thing. I was a bit more in my senses by then, but I have to admit I still didn't feel any overt motherly love. Neither did I cry seeing the baby or press him against my boobs.

I needn't have worried. The nurses did that. I am sure they see tits and vaginas all day long and so they forget these belong to people. A nurse walked in, untied my hospital gown briskly and plonked the baby on my chest. I was taken by surprise and so was my boy and my mother. Nani of course was very proud of the nurse, giving her approving looks of 'yes, yes, that's how it's done'.

Miraculously, the baby latched immediately, bringing the other six nurses into my room to come and stare at my magical breasts. It was making me very uncomfortable.

And if this wasn't enough, the next day when I woke up I saw a random mother with her baby standing by my bed. The nurses asked me if I could help this mother get her baby to latch by showing her how it was done. My boy laughed and excused himself from the room, but I refused to be an exhibit any more. I wished the mother good luck and asked her to leave.

My doctor saw this exchange and shook her head in disapproval. I was proving to be the worst mother out of her patients. I didn't seem to be into my kid, childbirth hadn't turned me into a being of soft, maternal generosity. But I couldn't fake it. My love for my baby took its own time to bloom. It wasn't an at-first-sight kind of thing. Instead, it grew every moment I spent with him. Intense, crazy love, mixed with worry, paranoia and, as I was to discover, a lot of guilt . . .

The First Sin

Sex

I was excited, guilty, happy, sad, all rolled into one. I was the typical Indian girl who is always guilty about things that give her joy.

I did my 'cowly' duties with utmost sincerity for six months, but I was determined not to go beyond that. My whole clan judged me. I was of course compared to my mother who had breastfed me for one whole year. There were also snide mentions of a distant (and obnoxious) cousin whose four-year-old twins were still dangling at her breasts.

She had come for dinner once with her twins to see the new baby. Her kids ran around the house playing catch and when they felt thirsty, they ran to their mom, pulled up her T-shirt, had a slurp or two of their favourite drink and got back to playing. She had become so lazy that all she did when the boys came to her was cover her breasts with the cushion lying next to her.

I was aghast and headed inside to make mashed potatoes for my six-and-a-half-month-old son. This did it for her and I was shamed subliminally the entire evening. I started feeling badly about myself, my decision to stop feeding and my lack of milk production (as it wasn't enough for the baby). I had not told anyone that within three months I had also started topping the baby's feed with formula for the nights. It was the guilty, dirty secret that I kept from the rest of the world.

To add to all this I had had an 'unnatural' caesarean and not a 'normal', vaginal delivery. If our clothes, the length of our hair, skin colour, work and marriage choices don't give people enough ammunition to judge us, now we can add our delivery options and feeding choices to the list. And god forbid if you choose not to have kids . . . ha, you are a goner.

That evening I felt miserable about myself. My mother sensed it. When our guests left, she told me to own my decision – to 'own it and with pride'. Yea man, enough of this crap.

But owning it with pride had two different meanings for my mother and me. What I did next turned into the family scandal. I planned a three-day trip to Bangkok with my boy and – hold your breath – without my seven-month-old baby.

My parents supported me and took care of the baby who was going to be completely weaned off once I was gone. I put the manual expressing machine to use and expressed a few bottles before leaving. I was excited, guilty, happy, sad, all rolled into one. I was the typical Indian girl who is always guilty about things that give her joy.

As soon as I reached the airport, my mother called me to say that the baby was fine and had already finished the bottles I had expressed. Oh no, what was I going to do? How was my baby going to survive? As I tried to pull out the expressing machine from my bag, my boy gave an incredulous look and said, 'No, you can't express another bottle, we are about to check in.'

Remembering the promise I made to myself, I took a deep breath, squeezed the boy's hand and told my mother that the baby would manage. And he did. We sat in the flight and were feeling giddy in love all over again. That's what a long-distance relationship does to you. But there was another less sexy current running through the honeymoony feeling.

I was still lactating and had to excuse myself to the lavatory to express a couple of times. Each time I expressed and threw the milk into the sink, I'd cry. F*ck you, prolactin, you didn't drop; screw you, dopamine, you didn't emerge; and the hell with all you aunties who made me feel guilty. You were winning.

The sexy bra I had worn for the trip proved to be really uncomfortable too. I had to stick ungainly breast pads into it to keep from leaking, which really spoiled the effect. F*ck, I miss my nursing bra, I said to myself after yet another trip to the bathroom and finally broke down in my seat. My boy tried to calm me and asked me why I was crying. All I could say at the time was that I was missing my nursing bra. Very unsexy, very un-Bangkok.

As I write this I am rolling my eyes at my insane, younger self. But I can still empathize with her. Like I said, in the self-esteem department, we women are a constant work in progress.

My boy wanted this trip to be memorable and really wanted to cheer me up. As soon as we landed we checked into our hotel and decided to explore the city. But before that I needed to express one more time. I was using a manual expressing pump. It's a contraption which has a plastic funnel that sticks to your boobs and is attached to a bottle.

You press a handle continuously (moms who have

used this will nod in agreement when I say you will get the best hand workout of your life using this pump, but to what end, who knows) and the milk collects in a bottle attached to the funnel – which in my case was to be thrown out (goddamn this guilt).

I went to the washroom and expressed but forgot to discard the milk. The prolactin had created a surge of maternal love in me. Missing my baby terribly, I headed out to call him. Yup, he was doing just fine. And now I felt a tinge of jealousy and worry. Why wasn't my son missing me? Of course if he had been I would be doubly miserable!

I kept the phone down and went back to the washroom to find the bottle empty. My boy was relaxing in the bedroom, having his protein shake. I asked him about the curious case of the missing breast milk and he smirked while chugging his shake and wiping his milk moustache.

'What?! Did you just drink it?' His only response was that it had the perfect temperature, was highly nutritious and blended perfectly with his protein shake. Yikes!

Now I have seen porn where men have sex with lactating women and squeeze their milk all over their faces. But this real-life version was far from horny. It felt like incest! Of course it wasn't, but it felt like it.

My boy was already living up to his promise of making this trip memorable! Now each time I had to express during the trip, I hid the bottle from the gym-going, protein shake–drinking, breast milk–stealing freak.

This milk business had thrown me off-kilter and I needed to get back into the groove. Maybe we needed to watch something stimulating? We ended up going for the ping-pong show. For the uninitiated, this was a live porn circus. The women were performing stunts with their cunts that I could have never imagined.

The show was mind-blowing. I had never known that the humble vagina could pop ten table-tennis balls at the audiences as well as rearrange the order and colour of the balls. If that wasn't enough, there were also moves with ribbons, Christmas tree decorations, a cup, spoons, even mismatched socks.

The mighty clit was carrying balls on a string, and the men were banging the girls in positions that the Kamasutra would feel embarrassed about. The orgasms were louder than the naaras of the protesters at Anna Hazare's anshan. Our eyes were wide in amazement.

But we were more scarred than turned on. I was just short of puking my guts out when one of the talented ladies threw a rattler at me from her indomitable vagina. Of all things, a baby rattler? The universe was conspiring against me. My boy told me it was a musical instrument, but I was convinced and completely stressed out.

I didn't end up using any of the new lingerie I had bought for the trip. Instead of making crazy love to each other we went to a shopping mall and did four hours of baby shopping. Soon it was time to take the flight home. As we sat in the aircraft our deprived eyes met, acknowledging all that had and hadn't happened. Mission unaccomplished.

We broke into laughter. As our flight took off and we put on our seat belts, our hands brushed against each other. It was electrifying. Soon our hands had found a life of their own; they knew each other's travel routes too well.

We took off quite literally. The seat belt sign went off. We headed to the lavatory one after the other and soon became members of the legendary mile-high club. Mission well accomplished!

The Second Sin

Guilt

That moment I realized I was nowhere close to being a perfect mother and that I was set on a path to make many blunders. This was just the beginning.

One of the first things I did as a new mom was turn my baby blue. Having brought him home from the nursing home I wanted to take complete charge of his well-being. I had read many books on pregnancy to prepare myself. In fact, I could have done a thesis on the subject. But when it comes to babies, theory never marries practice.

Soon it was time for him to have his first bath. Now my little boy was born in the biting cold winter of Chandigarh. So Dad and I warmed up the room with our classic old heater – not the fancy oil ones that we get today – while I got all the bath things ready. We thought we were prepared enough and took the baby's clothes off as gently as possible.

Almost immediately the poor thing started turning blue. Now this hadn't come up in any of my pregnancy books. Puzzled, I asked Dad if that's what babies usually did. My father's freaked-out face gave me my answer. I instantly wrapped the baby up in layers. That moment I realized I was nowhere close to being a perfect mother and that I was set on a path to make many blunders. This was just the beginning.

My second blunder was deciding not to get a full-time maid or nanny for the baby. I wanted to be absolutely hands-on. A few friends had recommended getting a 'jhaapa'. These are trained nannies usually from Kolkata, who are experts in childcare and stay with the new mom for around three months.

I had half a mind to agree, but I wanted to redeem myself for not having a 'regular' vaginal birth. Yes, even though no one in my immediate vicinity held me guilty for having a caesarean delivery, it's just understood that women who give birth the 'normal' way deserve society's medal.

I wanted that medal of being a perfect, brave mother too and so I declined any help for him. Of course, soon I went bonkers with the routine of bathing, massaging, feeding and burping.

I had only one magic weapon – good old mama's milk. A few slurps and it knocked out the baby for two hours straight. Two hours may not seem much to you, but ask any mom and she'll tell you it feels like heaven.

Guilt

Every time the kid went off to sleep, my body would slump in relief. I would manage to have a bath, eat, sleep, do a few errands and be ready again like a cow to be milked. Thank god babies getting drunk on their feed is a known phenomenon, otherwise the narcotics bureau would be after every mom.

Seeing how crazy and robotic I had become, my parents encouraged me to go for a quick coffee with my friends during one of the baby's post-milk naps. I could have used those precious hours to catch up on sleep but I was desperate to see faces that were not of my parents, the baby or the dog.

My younger girlfriends (without husbands and babies) came to pick me up, and as always I was hard-pressed for time. That day the little one decided to take a few more slurps, along with a bit more time to burp. I've always believed kids are sadists. I could feel the kid holding on to his burp, teasing his exhausted mom.

After completing all my mommy duties I rushed out to my friends who had been patiently waiting for the past twenty-five minutes in the car. It was great to have non-baby conversations. But as soon as we zipped past my lane, over a speed breaker I realized I had forgotten to put on my bra after the feed.

I pleaded with them to turn back, but they had lost all patience. My friend Guneet assured me, 'They aren't looking bad at all,' and that if we delayed any more, we'd never have our coffee.

We reached a Barista outlet and ordered our shakes and coffees. As we chatted away, we saw a good-looking boy checking us out. He didn't seem slimy either. We soon realized he was looking at me, and I have to admit it felt great. I know all about self-love, but if validation comes from a good-looking boy you feel doubly nice about yourself.

The boy got up from his table and began to walk towards us. 'Guess someone hasn't lost the touch,' teased one of my other friends. All of us were smiling; I was mentally preparing thank you notes for his compliments and thinking of a gentle way to tell him I was committed (yea, married; yea, fine, a mother). As he neared our table, he looked intently at me and then his eyes travelled to my chest. He gasped and did an about-turn and walked away.

Guneet nudged me. 'Bro, you are leaking.' I looked down at my T-shirt. Running down the front were two parallel streaks of milk. I began to cry in solidarity with my breasts. 'Let's just go home,' I told my friends.

Guilt

My sweetheart friends – my unmarried friends with no motherly feelings – saved the afternoon. No way, they said. We're not cutting this trip short. Let's go bra shopping! I still hadn't bought myself those maternity bras, the ones with a flap that you can pull down to feed the baby. I didn't even know these guys had heard of such a thing.

We walked into the mom-and-kids store and my pals checked out this whole new universe as I picked my bras. They were by now totally put off with all the milking, mommy, bra business. I teased them saying, 'You guys can buy these ones too. I bet they'd be useful in the winter to get some action. You won't have to take all your clothes off in the cold. Just a play of the flap you know!' They rolled their eyes and said, 'Babe, you should get some action!'

At home while trying on my new bras (the store managers refused to let me try anything seeing my T-shirt), I thought about what they said. Action was missing as my boy was shooting and travelling across the country. But that didn't mean I couldn't be adventurous on my own. Hmm . . .

I walked into the bathroom, locked both the doors to it and got ready for some loving exploration. No sooner did my hand find my nether regions than I heard my mother shouting from outside the bathroom, 'The baby has been farting non-stop, and the poop is very liquidy. Did you eat too much junk?'

Then came a knock on the door from my father. 'Beta, I am going to the market to get Digene and Eno for you; do you want anything else?' I was tempted to scream back, 'Haan, thodi shanti aur ek–do vibrator bhi le aao.' Well, there goes my paradise. I washed my hands and went back to the baby.

~

Exhausted by this completely baby-centred life, I decided I needed a break. I would take the baby back home to Mumbai to test the waters there and see if we liked it enough to settle in the city. Once I started packing I realized the few-months-old baby had more stuff than what three adults would carry.

I wore a blue poncho on the flight, one that covered all my curves and my belly. I had read that babies cry and feel pain in their ears while take-off and landing, and that one had to feed them then to ease the pressure. The poncho would come in handy as a cover-up for the baby.

I took my seat, settled him under the poncho and let him relish his favourite drink. A gentleman in his mid-fifties sat next to me. We exchanged pleasantries and got talking about his business. It was thrilling to have an adult conversation again. All I seemed to talk to my parents about was burps, spit-ups and diaper rashes. My son had his fill and dozed off. He slept the whole flight, cosy under the poncho, without moving an inch.

As soon as we landed, the gentleman extended his business card towards me just as I was taking the baby out from under the poncho. My co-passenger dropped the card in horror and looked at me as if I had just produced a baby on the flight. He got up and hurried away as quickly as he could, guilt written large on his face.

I picked up the card, on which he had written: 'Would love to take you for dinner ;)' What did that wink mean? I had given off no flirtatious vibes – all I had wanted was to have a conversation that didn't involve analysing the consistency of my baby's poop and then altering my diet according to it. Aaah, the wonders of breast milk – it wasn't just a miracle food but also a creep repellent.

As I stepped out of the airport, I saw one of my closest friends, Neeti, with balloons and the works.

It felt nice to be welcomed. My boy was shooting at that time. Today I can see why he needed to work and honour his commitments. But I would be lying if I say that at that point I understood and wasn't missing him. However, Neeti made me feel special and I have so much of gratitude for that.

I reached home and settled in but Mumbai was way too busy for a small-town girl with a workaholic husband and who had just had a baby. I thought perhaps losing weight would help me feel better about things. I was stupid and I own it. Some people learn the hard way, and I guess I am one of them.

And so, though I was feeding the baby, I started eating less and working out more. I would take him in his pram to the gym when it was usually empty to burn off those extra kilos. Sometimes the baby observed me as I huffed and puffed on the treadmill. Sometimes, wanting to play, he would look at his freak of a mom, then fall asleep in boredom.

I felt guilty about not playing with him when he wanted to despite the fact that I was stuck to him for practically twenty-four hours a day. I felt guilty about gaining twenty-two kilos when he weighed a mere two and a half kilos.

Guilt

I felt guilty when anyone asked me how much the baby weighed and being judged for it. I felt guilty about trying to beat the weight while feeding. I felt guilty about the top feed I had started giving him. I felt guilty about having someone to help me with the baby. I felt guilty about getting back to work. It was guilt, guilt, guilt, 24/7.

And if in that zone you see your partner spending joyous time with the baby and not feeling guilty about anything at all, not only do you feel like stabbing him but you also come up with torturous ways of doing so.

My friends were wonderful. Watching me struggle, they organized a lunch at the Westin Hotel nearby. I was meeting them after a long time and was really looking forward to it.

I dressed the baby in his nicest clothes, packed everything he could possibly need for a whole week and tucked him in his pram. Feeling very confident and happy, I picked up the designer handbag that I hadn't used for so long. I had shed some weight and was already fitting into my pre-pregnancy clothes.

I got to the restaurant and parked the pram beside my chair. The baby was sleeping comfortably. His first lunch outing was turning out to be a real success. There was good food and company and fun conversation.

It's always a bit stressful to go into the world after a baby and get back in sync with the latest news and all the buzz. Like any new mom my head was full of sleeplessness and diapers, and I had no idea about the latest films, IPL results or the new political scandal.

I leapt in, trying to keep up. I had to be this cool mom, who was fit, who knew everything, was a great conversationalist and was just perfect.

Once lunch was over I hugged each of my friends, and headed to the elevator. Just then one of the staff members came running towards me, putting his foot in the door before it shut. 'Madam,' he said, 'you have forgotten your baby!'

Everyone in the lift gave me a look I will never forget. People forget to pay bills or leave their bag behind. I forgot my baby even though I was still holding on to my bag. What kind of cruel mother does that? So much for trying to be the best, I had simply ended up on my favourite journey – a guilt trip.

I haven't stopped making mistakes. From dropping the kids to school on a public holiday, to giving them the wrong dose of medicine, to putting on the baby's diaper the wrong way, to wearing the wrong-coloured

Guilt

T-shirt on sports day and supporting the rival team instead, to missing Zoom birthday parties – my list of blunders is endless. Some things haven't changed, but one thing has – today I am more forgiving of myself!

The Third Sin

Infidelity

And now suddenly, after all those years, I began to think about him. Perhaps it was the attention, the butterflies in my stomach that I was missing, or perhaps it was just the idea of falling in love that had struck me anew.

I think I had my midlife crisis pretty early. I was thirty-two and my second baby was just a year old. Perhaps it was the desire to be wanted, getting some validation, wanting to feel like an attractive twenty-year-old again or the result of back-to-back pregnancies and all the childcare. Something was amiss, because I began to obsessively look for a boy who had had the hots for me in school.

He was one of the most good-looking boys in our batch. One of my friends was crazy about him; another one used to make crank calls to him. I kept him on tenterhooks for around a year and a half, like a cheap version of Poo from *Kabhi Khushi Kabhie Gham*. I enjoyed all the attention I got from him but never had a relationship with him.

Our souls just didn't connect. At seventeen, with raging hormones, one usually doesn't think about soul connections, but I just couldn't do it. I have to admit though that when he moved on, I missed all the attention.

The two-hour-long phone calls, his heroic entry in my class just to check me out, the way he would ensure I sat next to him by getting all the other seats blocked, waiting for me with his group of friends in front of the tuition centre, complimenting me for the smallest things, like my nail colour.

He was a charmer, I'll give him that. Had I not enjoyed the attention, I wouldn't have entertained all his herogiri. And now suddenly, after all those years, I began to think about him. Perhaps it was the attention, the butterflies in my stomach that I was missing, or perhaps it was just the idea of falling in love that had struck me anew.

I began to look for him on Facebook. He didn't seem to be on it. I tried all the permutations of his name. No luck. Each time I did this, I felt terribly guilty and quickly shut the laptop. But the next day I would again look for him on Instagram.

After many failed attempts, I felt not just belittled but also irritated with myself. I couldn't believe what I was doing. And what amped the annoyance was disbelief at him not having any social media presence whatsoever. How could that be?

I didn't have any way to trace him except through one person. And that person was my boy, as he was part of the class WhatsApp group and this guy was my boy's batchmate and friend. Urghhh. The irony. But what do I tell my boy? Why did I need his number? Especially when he knew our history too well.

I picked up my boy's phone when he wasn't around. I didn't know his password, so I am not even sure what I was thinking. But some dark instinct had made me pick up his phone, give it a try. Almost as soon as I picked it up, I dropped it in disgust. This was the lowest I had fallen. People pick up their partner's phone to check whether they are cheating, not to cheat themselves!

I waited for my boy to come out of the loo. As soon as he did I blurted out the guy's name and asked for his number straight up. So I hadn't fallen low enough to get the number on the sly, but hadn't risen high enough to let go either.

My boy was taken aback. I think he would have given me the number, but the fact that I was behaving like the aggressive BSF soldiers patrolling the Wagah border made him think twice. He asked me what my intention was. Did I even know? I shrugged my shoulders and didn't give an answer.

My boy thought I had lost it, and we dropped the subject. But the next day I was standing outside the bathroom with the same question. He too asked the same question as the previous day. And I had the same reply. Nothing.

The next day he stepped out of the bathroom wary of being accosted by a mad woman. This time I surprised him by popping out from behind his cupboard. I thought perhaps a change in position might lead to a different result.

The week went by like this until I had a meltdown. I couldn't believe what I was doing – throwing a fit in front of my husband to get the number of a guy from my past, and for what? I didn't know! He didn't budge. But I couldn't stop myself.

Eventually the intensity of my feelings subsided. I had days of irrationality, but they were punctuated now by many days of calm. Nope, it wasn't because I started getting special attention from my boy or that he began to compliment me on my nail colour.

I could get my hair coloured pink and he would still be worried about Mumbai's AQI. I just tried to make an effort to love myself a bit more. I would still have off days, but now at least there were good days too.

My phone buzzed on one of those fleeting good days. I picked it up to see that my boy had shared a contact with me. It was that guy's number. It was what I had been searching for all this time. But what was I supposed to do with it now? I saved the number.

Very hesitantly I typed out a 'hi' to him. There was a quick 'hi' back. Then I froze. The awkward silence was filled by me sending something inane like 'Appliances get rusty quite quickly in Mumbai, there is a lot of humidity here. I need to go. Will get back to you.' I left it there.

Picking up the phone on someone after fifteen years and talking about Mumbai's humidity perhaps wasn't the most romantic opening line. Neither did our exchange leave my heart racing. There was a void in me, and talking to him hadn't filled it.

I learnt only to fill it a few years on, when I realized the only one missing in my life was me. That was the void. Of course all our relationships count and are a big blessing, but it really takes you to be your own biggest cheerleader to feel complete.

Then three years ago, the only boy who had a

persistent crush on me in school messaged me out of the blue. At school I had friend-zoned him. I was a bit of a late bloomer, my hormones mostly in hibernation, and I had genuinely liked him as a friend. We all eventually moved on. I got married and had two kids and he got married and had a kid too.

But that day when I got a cryptic message from him, I realized this midlife crisis (hitting us in our early thirties instead of our fifties) was gender-neutral. I knew it was momentary. A temporary feeling that clouds you when you are at your lowest.

Love and relationships can't be formed at your lowest. I didn't get offended. I wrote to him instead to say I understood what he was going through and tried to schedule a call with him to help him understand.

But before the call could happen, I was detected with breast cancer. I guess the news must have scared him off as I received no call or message thereafter. But I really hope he reads this book and knows that it's never too late to fall in love with yourself.

Not a Sin, but a Confession

Submission

They kept taking digs at me for wearing the same clothes. What if my English was weak, what if I truly didn't have more clothes? Was that something to be held against me?

This is going to be a tough one to write. Bullying. This is a story about me as a child, but I think it holds some important lessons for all us parents.

My middle-class parents had some rich family friends. There was no rich or poor divide among the adults, but the same can't be said when it came to the kids. Now they have probably turned out to be great as adults, but as kids, gosh, they were quite mean to me.

Every Saturday, for about five years of my childhood, from the ages of five or six to eleven, my parents would visit them for their family get-togethers. I would tag along and get picked on each time.

I used to plead with my parents not to take me to those parties. I can't blame my parents. It was a break for them after working so hard the entire week. The couples had been their friends since university days.

What a lovely bond they had! I wished I could achieve an iota of that with their kids. And so with teary eyes and a clenched jaw, I would enter their palatial home to give it another try – only to fail miserably.

I don't know what led to the attacks, but they certainly had a privilege that I didn't. I wondered at one point if they were picking on me because I was a single kid, but nope, there were other single kids too. Whatever the reason, I was the chosen one.

Kids can be very mean. To an eight- or nine-year-old, a mean kid is as scary as a dragon. Most evenings were made up of eleven to twelve kids, some younger and some older. And every week I had to face the malice of these twelve dragons. Pushing and shoving was basic. It was often far uglier.

One night we were playing hide-and-seek in the dark. Usually the 'den' was selected with a quick game of 'rock, paper, scissors' or the desi version, 'pugan ka pugata'. But in this case I was of course made the den.

Now Chandigarh houses are big and this one was especially so. I was in the lawn in the pitch-dark night. I kept searching for them, getting more and more scared with each passing minute. The sound of crickets and bats in the background began to seem like the cries of monsters. I could have peed myself in fear.

Crying was absolutely not allowed, neither was going inside to my folks. And what if the kids saw me and thought I was weak! Ha, stupid me, they already knew. I was submissive to another level, and this also comes from a place I'll touch upon later.

I don't know how long I was outside. It may have been minutes which felt like hours, it may have been an hour. I finally went inside and found them watching TV and laughing their guts out when they saw me. I silently took my place in the corner of the room, trying to disappear.

Another evening my mother decided to put my hair in two ponytails. I had very long hair, and I thought I looked good. Perhaps this will help me win over those monsters, I thought to myself. And voila, what happens next? After an evening of making fun of me, one of them began to pull hard at my ponytails. I winced in pain, but she didn't let up.

The others laughed. I was deeply hurt seeing their faces. What was so funny seeing another kid in pain? Even though I was taller, perhaps stronger than my tormentor (in fact, she was a year younger to me), not a word came out of my mouth. And so it went on till the brat wanted a break and a Coke. The game had got her tired and thirsty, you see.

At school I was the captain of co-curricular activities. I aced it all, be it elocution or drama. But here in this hard, real world I couldn't utter a word. In fact, fear and nervousness would often leave me tongue-tied in front of these kids. One day I said something in incorrect English because of my timidity. The bullies of course jumped on my mistake and corrected me mockingly. I tried to redeem myself and said, 'Sorry, slip . . . tongue,' which made them laugh even harder.

The bullying made me start stammering a bit at that time.

They weren't uniformly awful. One of the kids had some empathy. On one occasion I saw the gang two days in a row. I had recently got a purple-coloured pair of Garfield shorts and T-shirt that I was very excited about. So I wore the outfit on both days.

After all, we do repeat vegetables or leftover dal from the night before, and this was a new set of clothes for me. But these kids! They kept taking digs at me for wearing the same clothes. What if my English was weak, what if I truly didn't have more clothes? Was that something to be held against me?

I decided then that I would never ever judge others on the basis of their clothes, speech or background.

In fact, when I started dating my boy at eighteen, he couldn't speak two straight lines of English without saying 'had' instead of 'have'. And I never judged him. Instead, I helped him speak the correct way.

That day I retreated as usual to a corner and a girl my age came to me and asked gently, 'Why did you repeat?' I had a simple answer. 'I love Garfield and these are new clothes that I got last month.' She smiled. I saw that she understood. Today she is a good friend.

Eventually, as luck would have it, our parents had differences and the group split. Woohoooooooo!!!! I can't begin to tell you how much I celebrated that first Saturday I didn't have to go to a party! I felt a little bad for my folks for losing out on good friends, but for myself I was exhilarated.

I regained my confidence. I flourished. No more stammering, no more being judged. I made a new set of friends at school. Life became amazing once again. Having said that, the parents have all reunited now. I am extremely fond of them and I am really happy for them, for they found their friends back.

Today when I look back at the time, I can see the incidents for what they were. Mean-spirited, snobby bullying. At the time though, I felt I was to blame. Perhaps I brought out the worst in them for some reason. When I meet them now, they come across as polite, civilized adults.

In a kid's world, everything is exaggerated because that's how kids see things. Houses are bigger, cars look bigger, your seniors look bigger, everything is multiplied as your own size is small and so is your vision. In retrospect, I don't just question the behaviour of the bullies; I look back at my behaviour too. Why was I so submissive? Why couldn't I speak up?

The reason for this was something darker that I was experiencing during those years, which was eating away at me. I was abused as a child by someone close to the family. I didn't have the courage to speak up or tell my parents because I was scared. What was I so scared of? I don't know. I felt guilty at having brought this on myself, and it's from these tangled feelings that I learned the art of being submissive.

The bullies did not know what was going on in my life, but they could perhaps read into my submissive behaviour. Eventually, just like the bullying, the abuse too stopped on its own, though the pain of the latter can't be compared to the former. I always waited for some divine intervention. I never took action. I didn't know that I could take action, that I could say no.

I carried the hurt and pain of that experience into my adulthood.

I can't blame my parents. I have the heart of a parent today and it would kill me to know my child went through such an experience, and as I write this, I know including this chapter of my life will hurt them. But that's why I am writing – I am both a parent and a kid here.

Can I use my experience to keep my kids safe? Is there anything I can tell you to help you? Like most of you, I have introduced the concept of bad and good touch to my kids. I try to be alert, but I know from terrible experience that no one can predict anything.

Nonetheless, here are my learnings. You can of course be vigilant, but I am not sure it is possible to micromanage every moment of the child's life. I am not a fan of helicopter parenting. Instead, I believe that communication lines should be open between parents and kids. I have encouraged mine to be honest, often to my detriment (see the seventh sin).

Kids learn to keep secrets and their thoughts to themselves early on. My approach is never to ask questions about what they are up to if I feel they are being defensive. Instead, I ask them about their friends and school when they are relaxed, like when we are in bed reading a story or while painting. My first instinct is also not to blame them or scold them but to try and learn the backstory of why they committed a mistake. Children clam up when they feel the parent is stressed or upset.

We can't prevent abuse but we might have the power to catch it early on if we talk about it. I couldn't speak of it as a child and the burden of silence was its own prison. I feel the rate of abuse might reduce or perhaps get reported more often if we start talking about it.

Kids are affected not only by the communication they have with their parents but also by all the communication they see in the world around them. How does the world treat victims and perpetrators? How is the news being reported? What kind of shame is associated with confessing?

Children start understanding the workings of the world from a young age. They are more perceptive than us. Another tip that I got from a friend was to show your vulnerable side to your kids. It is okay to admit to a mistake, it is okay to blunder as a parent.

Your kids will see you falling but they will also see you gathering your wits and rising again. Our children tend to hero-worship us but if we can let go of our guard and be mere mortals, perhaps our fall and rise will inspire them to confess to something they are holding on to.

And if unfortunately you have gone through something as a kid, please release those feelings. You are not guilty. That's all I wanted to hear in my life.

I finally told my boy after the birth of our son. I didn't know what his reaction would be. I thought he might hold me accountable for it. Of course he didn't. He held me close and I could see his pain. His love and acceptance of my past opened up all the feelings I had bottled up for so long. I cried and cried and cried. It was the first time I had cried about my abuse.

Till then there had been only anger, guilt and sadness. As the tears rolled down my cheeks, the weight of my past became lighter. Then I told my parents. They were crushed. My mother especially was devastated. She confronted the man and broke all ties with him – an act of courage that made me so proud of her.

This was the first time I spoke out. The second was when Barkha Dutt interviewed me and asked a question about my childhood. I struggled for words and she understood my silence instinctively. She too had undergone a similar experience. Each time I have shared this, I have come back feeling lighter.

We have to talk, and we have to free ourselves from our traumas. Parents, don't feel guilty that you couldn't protect your kids. No parent would want that for their child. And if you are a victim, you too must free yourself from feelings of anger, remorse and guilt. These will only eat into you. One way of doing this is to express yourself.

Let's introduce our kids to empathy and compassion. Life will teach them the same lesson, but it's never too early to start. We should also teach them that they aren't to blame for sexual abuse. Shame and guilt are for the perpetrator.

Ultimately, and above all, we have to speak up, so that our kids learn that they have the power to speak up too. Perpetrators should be held accountable and called out. Why am I not calling out mine here? Because my mom did that. And she is my hero.

The Fourth Sin

Tyranny

The young woman's beautiful eyes widened in horror as she inhaled the fumes emanating from our table. The couple quickly moved away and took a table on the other side of the room.

My second pregnancy was like my first one only in speed and the accidental way in which I got knocked up. In every other way, I was a different me. During my second pregnancy I got back to life with a vengeance, made a short film (which I didn't have the guts to show anyone, it's still with me), co-authored (ahem) a book with my boy and directed a play based on my second book.

We staged two shows each in Chandigarh and Delhi while I was nauseous, throwing up and making life miserable for everyone around me. I was a far cry from a pious pregnant lady and showed no remorse or empathy for those who committed mistakes during workshops. I strongly expressed what I wanted, vehemently shared my opinions and then I popped a girl. A little feisty girl who reflected some of those energies of the pregnancy.

With baby one, I had learnt my lesson about trying to do it all by myself. So with baby two I decided to try out the legendary jhappas. The first lady who came from Kolkata had a simple condition – she would sleep when the baby slept and would only work for the hours the baby was awake. Now a newborn sleeps for up to seventeen hours in a day and is barely awake for hours at a stretch. I had to let her go.

The next one was very active and all knowledgeable. She said she'd delivered a baby at a very famous family's home. She was longing for me to be nosy and ask her questions, but I was too harried to be curious.

That didn't stop her. She would start talking about the extremely affluent family where she helped the mother and the newborn every chance she got. While she prepared the massage table for the baby she threw in the word 'Mumbai', and while burping the baby she dropped another hint – Bollywood.

My patience eventually ran out. I asked her whom she had worked for. I saw her triumphant, gleeful smile as I gave in. She whispered, 'The Bachchans.' I was taken aback, and had to reconfirm, 'You mean

Shehenshah Bachchan? Bunty–Babli Bachchan? KBC Bachchan?' With each question my decibel rose.

She gave me a look. 'I am worth it wali Bachchan.' Of course I was very impressed. But then almost immediately came the thought that she would judge my humble abode in Chandigarh after having spent months in Prateeksha or Jalsa.

The woman was truly relentless. She started bragging about how she could help a mother get her glow back and talking about the face packs that she had used on the moms she had worked for. Soon she had taken full charge of the baby. I didn't like being away from my baby, but I was such a pushover.

She would intimidate me with her knowledge and past experience, and I started feeling incompetent as a mother. I doubted my sensibility and way of doing things and questioned my decisions. Then I started having doubts about her. Eventually I had to ask her to leave. Later I checked with the agency about her profile. And madam hadn't ever even set foot in Mumbai, let alone treat Aishwarya Rai Bachchan's skin!

Scarred by this experience I took even more time filling her role. Finally came Rupa didi, a sweet lady in her mid-forties from Kolkata. She was warm and helpful and all smiles. The only drawback was that she couldn't speak Hindi. And I couldn't understand Bengali. But we clicked.

She was a big foodie, perhaps that's why we connected. But when it came to eating, I was a rookie next to her. She ate round the clock and loved to feed my two-year-old son too. I practically had to stop her from making him eat so much – which mom has ever confessed to that sin?

We moved to Mumbai. Mom, two kids, the jhappa. Slowly we began to settle into our life there. Soon my toddler son was reciting poems in Bangla. He started getting a Bengali accent too, heck, my few-months-old daughter was also crying in a different accent! I always wanted my kids to be multilingual, but I have to admit I was an insecure mother.

My sin was that I couldn't let go of my kids. If they learnt something new or different from others, I would feel a pang of jealousy. So one day I decided to let Rupa didi chill at home and order in pizzas for her while I took my two kids to Starbucks in Andheri to spend quality time with them alone.

I ordered a coffee and pastry. I made them write my son's name on the cup and had them call out his name when the order was ready. He was thrilled that the staff at a random coffee shop knew his name. I chuckled to myself and let this memory be etched in my heart forever. As I was engaged in conversation with my kids, a cool-looking young couple walked into the coffee shop and were about to occupy the table next to us. They smiled seeing the kids and me.

Just then Rupa didi's magic worked on my son. Nope, he didn't start speaking in Bangla, but instead let out a silent, toxic, pungent, deathly fart. The young woman's beautiful eyes widened in horror as she inhaled the fumes emanating from our table. The couple quickly moved away and took a table on the other side of the room. I wanted to apologize but that would have made things worse!

I guess the coffee shop was a jinxed place for me. But despite this slightly embarrassing moment, it turned out to be a fun outing. I went back home with my ducklings in tow and a smile on my face.

As I entered my apartment, I sniffed the air. Rupa didi was smiling, waiting for us in the living room, and surrounding her was that same bloody smell. I didn't have the guts to confront her on her and my son's gaseous emissions but I did make sure that only I fed my son from that day on.

Luckily for me, Rupa didi had to leave. She suffered from severe back pain. The greater her discomfort, the more smelly garlic and turmeric concoctions she consumed. And the more severe her gaseous emissions became. I too would be sore from the pain she caused to my olfactory system.

I was on the verge of collapsing when she said she should take a break. I was more than happy to let her go and, yes, I am guilty of never asking her to come back.

Now I was without a nanny again. And the one thing I had learnt with baby two was that love them or loathe them, the nanny–mom relationship was one for keeps. This was the tyranny they imposed upon you.

In my quest to find the perfect nanny and to entertain my kids, I often went to the play area of my building. There I met Komal, my soul sister. We instantly bonded over our love for La Senza double-padded bras and our relationship with our nannies.

Komal's nanny loved giving moral, religious and even physiological lessons to Komal's three-year-old daughter. Once her daughter had pointed to the nanny's bra and asked her what it was. The nanny, without missing a beat, had responded that they were 'attachments' women had. I guess pretty much like the extra attachments you get with nerf guns. Blame it on her vocabulary or her way of evading the question.

One night Komal was unhooking her bra, letting the load off her chest if you think about the crazily padded bras we all have to carry around the whole day. Her daughter who was in the room screamed in horror. 'Mama's attachments have broken, Daddy, come quick. They have fallen!'

The education didn't stop there. On another occasion the kid asked the nanny why the boys in her class peed standing. The good woman told her that the boys had a pipe. At school the little girl accidentally opened a loo door while her classmate was on the pot. In horror she ran back to her classroom, saying loudly, 'Dhruv's pipe is broken, it needs to be fixed.' The teacher was flabbergasted and immediately summoned the poor parents for counselling.

I had asked Komal if her nanny could help find me a nanny. Komal said she was too fond of me to do such a thing. I was torn. What was better – no nanny or hiring a relative of this madcap? I was desperate enough to contemplate a Mary Poppins who would teach my kids about broken pipes and detachable equipment. The only thing worse than a crazy nanny was no nanny at all.

The Fifth Sin

Obscenity

His smile seemed to say, I won't let anyone judge you, I got your back, Mommy. Some equations of the heart can never be understood.

Shit shit shit shit shit . . . no, that was not a typo. That was my two-year-old son trying out this cool new word he had heard slip out of my mouth. In normal circumstances he would have tried it out a few times and soon forgotten all about it. But because I had freaked out, the sadist made it his life's mission to go around saying the word for days.

The more I got irked, the more he said it. Thankfully, he did forget about it after a few days. Lesson learnt: the more you react to a kid's bad behaviour, the greater the chances of them continuing with it. But the problem is that parenting wisdom is so much easier in theory than practice.

A few weeks later I think I pricked my hand or was talking excitedly with a friend on the phone, and casually dropped a 'f*ck'. Next thing I know 'f*ck f*ck f*ck f*ck f*ck f*ck f*ck' is all I hear from this crazy three-foot kid. He went to town with that one. Now it's not that I had completely forgotten my lesson. I didn't scold or correct him. When it comes to observation and emotional instincts, kids are worlds apart from adults. I guess we lose these skills when we grow up.

My son didn't get a scolding from me, but he didn't have to. He knew he had hit the bullseye when he saw my horrified expression. That's all the little monster needed. Lesson learnt again. Zip your mouth and get yourself Botoxed. But before I attained this wisdom, I had to face some humiliations.

We were in Chandigarh. It was lovely to see my mother bond with her grandson. She would return from a hectic day at school and greet him the same sweet way every day – squatting low and opening her arms wide, so he could dive into them. That day wasn't any different, except the hug ended with him looking at his nani, moon-eyed, and saying 'f*ck'.

Mama was mortified. Oh no Mama, I thought to myself. That reaction is fodder for this lamb. My son looked at her in wicked glee. He began to run around in circles, saying 'f*ck' louder and louder. I tried to catch him and shut him up but it was all just too much fun for him.

At night when Dad came back from work, he too was greeted by his favourite grandchild's welcoming word. My father was shocked but he had been in many embarrassing situations earlier too, thanks to me, and had learnt the fine art of ignoring. I saw the disappointment in my son's eyes. Yesss . . . that was a sixer, Dad!

Next day the mali bhaiya came. My son loved gardening and was maliji's permanent assistant. But that day their conversation sounded a bit different. Maliji couldn't understand baba's talk at all. 'Phuck, woh kya hota hai, beta? Dekhna tum ek din bade phankaar banoge.'

A few days later 'f*ck' became 'cluck', 'duck', 'muck', and finally 'suck'. Seriously? I would have made peace with it had it been 'luck' or something a little nicer. But no, 'suck' it was. I was on a call with my boy who was shooting in Delhi. We were back to being in a long-distance relationship, but there was magic in it too.

We longed for each other and indulged in a new phenomenon at that time called sexting and sex chats when we could. I prodded my boy, trying to be discreet. 'Baby, it's been so long, should we—' We were interrupted by 'suck suck suck suck suck suck suck'. What the f*ck!

My boy was shocked with the background music at my end. 'What are you teaching our son,' he asked angrily. 'No no, baby, he didn't say the f-word . . . it's just that . . . I muttered, trying to dig my way out of the hole. He retaliated with, 'Suck isn't any better,' and said he wasn't in the mood and put the phone down before we had even got to first base.

I looked at my toddler who was looking back at his dejected mother with dreamy eyes full of love and a big smile on his face. He opened his mouth again and as I was bracing myself, I heard him say 'muck'. I looked at him amazed, and relieved too. He smiled and went out of the room chanting 'muck muck muck'. His smile seemed to say, I won't let anyone judge you, I got your back, Mommy. Some equations of the heart can never be understood.

Like mother, like son

As I write this book about my kids and being a mom, I am reminded time and again of my own parents and what I was like as a kid. And the short answer is, not that different from our little monsters. My little guy might be a master of embarrassment, and he has got that from me. I spent my entire childhood mortifying my poor parents. Take this incident which is still laughed about at home.

I was five. It was a hot summer in Chandigarh, and one Sunday my parents invited some relatives over for lunch. The Chandigarh social scene consists of parents turning their kids into performing monkeys. So I was brought in to recite a poem.

When I was done, and praise was showered and claps were clapped, the conversation moved on to the next recurring topic – which was why my parents had only one kid and how they should have another one quickly. I had even been taken to a corner by one such relative to urge me to demand for a brother or a sister since it was my duty as a good daughter to do so.

Demand was the word. Looking back on those chats I now think, really? So at that lunch, everyone got after my poor mother as usual. I decided I had to do something and said loudly, 'Mama can't have kids.' All conversation stopped. Eyebrows were raised. Enjoying the attention, I told everyone, 'It's because Mama has nirodh, I have seen it in the ad.' I grew up in the dark ages when the whole family would watch television together. There were hardly any channels or shows, screen time was limited and there were few advertisements, which every child would know to sing along to.

This particular ad said that in order not to have more babies, you need to use nirodh. So my five-year-old brain translated that to 'if my mother isn't having more babies of course she is eating loads of nirodh!' Mama wanted to become Sita that day and disappear into the earth. Papa gulped and did his usual ostrich thing. My relatives didn't know where to look. Sigh . . . it was the longest lunch of our lives.

The Sixth Sin

Corruption

As soon as you have a kid, your beautiful haven of a bed, where you can relax, rest and recuperate, will be colonized by the monster. The second only makes it worse.

Having two kids in quick succession creates all kinds of complications. In fact, it has tangible effects on your well-being. I am talking about the takeover of your bed. As soon as you have a kid, your beautiful haven of a bed, where you can relax, rest and recuperate, will be colonized by the monster. The second only makes it worse.

Having read all the parenting blogs, I had made elaborate plans for the transition of my year-and-a-half-old toddler to sleep in his room. I made a real effort to decorate his room and got him a fancy pirate bed in our Mumbai flat. I'll have my life and my boy back, I said to myself gleefully.

Then we had another baby who naturally slept with us. The toddler wanted equal rights, and so the four of us ended up sleeping together. And the poor pirate bed was abandoned.

Longitudinally we wouldn't fit, so we squeezed ourselves latitudinally, pretty much like on an Indian railway platform. The romance for a couple of accidentally finding each other was not a possibility for us, as we were separated by two babies, pillows and what seemed to be an endless bed.

This couldn't be my life! I still have vivid memories of sharing my parents' room every summer as a kid because we had only one air conditioner. In the middle of the night I would notice those two tall beings sneak out of the room. I would fall back asleep until one day curiosity got the better of me. After pretending to be asleep for a while, I got up to go to the other room.

Thankfully all I saw was my mother trying to wear her nightie. She took it in her stride and said, 'I was just dusting this off. It has got ants on it.' A few years later the ant story made a different kind of sense to me, and the memory of it has some biting effects.

If I couldn't get my toddler into his own cot, I was convinced I'd end up with him in my bed forever and my marriage would be doomed. But forget the sex part, I just wanted to sleep peacefully without having my butt kicked and eyes poked every night.

I started devising ways to send the older one to his room. I scolded, explained, lost my temper, then cajoled. Nothing worked as it didn't make sense to him. 'We are supposed to sleep together like a team' was his response. But then how was I supposed to bench this team or, better still, manage to get myself disqualified?

Finally I tried the unethical way of bribing. I told him I would get him the fancy toy he had been asking for if he started sleeping in his room. It worked wonders, and I could finally sleep with a big grin.

But in life karma catches up, and it didn't require a sting operation to expose my corruption. All I needed was a few neighbours to come over for chai and my son running around and creating chaos. When I asked him to stop, he said, 'If you give me Lego, I'll stop.'

I gave him a stern look but it didn't register as he was too busy running his scooty over everyone's feet. Trying to cover up, I shrugged and smiled. 'Hehe . . . kids, you know what they are like, na?' Meanwhile, chai and snacks were being served along with milk for my son.

When I asked him to have it, the little monster said, 'If you give me candy, I'll drink milk.' I could feel the cold judgy vibes of the friendly neighbours and squirmed. I tried placating him the passive-aggressive way but nothing worked. Not wanting to make a fool of myself any further, I stopped nagging him.

As they were about to leave, I asked my son to wish them goodbye. Before he could open his mouth to say 'if you give me . . .', one of them asked me, 'Does he ask you for a bribe for everything?'

She said, somewhat smugly, that she had a three-year-old who had never resorted to such lowly acts. What?! I felt like digging out all the pakoras and cheese sandwiches from her stomach. Not so friendly, after all.

At that time, though, I felt so guilty about what she said that the only thing to come out of my mouth was a timid 'I guess to each their own'. They left, and I sat in the living room seething with embarrassment, anger and – let's admit it – shame. To each their own? What precedent had I set for myself?

What exactly was my own? Bribing? So much for all the moral lessons on character I had got from my father. I felt terrible. And I had no one to blame. My son was only echoing what I had taught him.

I had half a mind to teach him pretence, not to say such things in front of people.

But I couldn't teach him more corruption. Now I really had to undo what I had taught him. And the only way to do that was to have him come back to the room to sleep with us since I didn't want to bribe him further. That night I got relatively fewer kicks, perhaps my kid's way of showing gratitude.

I adopted another ploy – I would pick him up after he fell asleep and tuck him in his bed. But that was a bigger disaster as when I hit my sweet REM stage, the boy would crawl back in. Locking doors meant constant knocking, unlocked doors meant having him come right back like a delayed boomerang.

For a healthy adult they say around three to five REM cycles is good, and that finally deep sleep should be the goal. Of course, these adults don't include mothers. All studies should have a separate sample pool of mothers and carry out parallel studies for them. They can't be included in the regular adult group.

I started walking around like a zombie. Why wasn't my boy disturbed like me? Well, he can cuddle and sleep deeply while I can't have anyone even touch my toes, forget sharing a blanket. So of course I was the chosen sufferer. Sleeping in my son's room wasn't an option as the fancy single pirate bed I got made for him couldn't accommodate me.

The only other room in the home we had at that time was where our staff slept. I was tempted to crawl into their bed, but that would have probably creeped them out. And losing staff is the biggest fear for any mother who wants to have a life.

I resigned myself to my fate. Kicks, jabs and pokes were going to be a part of my cycle of sleep and there was nothing I could do about it.

One night my son and I were fooling around and I got into the pirate bed with him. It wasn't very comfortable, my feet were dangling out, but I saw he was feeling very secure. I picked up his favourite book and started reading to him. And just like that, he fell asleep in his room.

I had had no plans to put him to sleep but it worked! When I wasn't anxious, he responded. What was it all about then? Just being relaxed? No amount of reading on Google or talking to elders and paediatricians had helped me wean him off. It was just the energy I was giving out.

I would be lying if I say it became an everyday thing instantly. But we improved. Day by day, week after week. When my son not only heard but also felt that I wasn't pushing him away, that it was just a good habit to sleep on your own, he took to it happily.

The mom–kid relationship cannot have a rulebook. And I take back what I said about survey groups. Moms can't fall into any survey group. Just like every kid and the set of problems they pose are unique, every mom and her set of solutions are unique too!

The Seventh Sin

—

Indiscretion

The little one, who was playing with magna tiles next to us and stealing the makhanas meant for the guest, asked oh-so-innocently, 'What's masterburate?' What the freaking hell!

As my kids have grown older, I have stopped worrying about controlling their eating, sleeping and swearing. Now I just give them moral science lectures. I tell them that having compassion and inner goodness and being a caring human being are far bigger achievements than anything else. And, above all, it's important to always be honest and express one's feelings.

The seven- and nine-year-old pretend to listen to me seriously. But the other day the younger one sent me a note under the bathroom door saying, 'As much as we love your speeches about being good, Mama, we want you to follow them too.'

I knew where this was coming from. Miss Smarty Pants was trying to persuade me once again to let them meet their friends even as we are in the middle of the second wave of the Covid-19 pandemic and another lockdown. The poor kids haven't met anyone that looks like them in over a year. They see their friends only virtually through Zoom classes. It's a shame, I know.

This isn't the first note that's been slipped under the door. Ever since my daughter began to hold a crayon, she has been barraging me with SOS messages such as this one whenever I go to the loo. Sticking to me the whole day has never been enough for her; she even follows me into the bathroom.

As I sat on the pot, a piece of paper would slip in under the door. Sometimes there would be a picture of a sad smiley, at times a tree, at other times a picture of me that looked nothing less than a monster.

Then when she learnt writing, the drawings turned into notes. 'Why arr yoo tacing so long?' 'Wot arr yoo doing der?' What do you think I am doing! 'I wont to eet pasta' – while I am trying to evacuate last night's spaghetti. Nothing appetizing about these notes!

As she grew older, the notes got more pointed. Once she even wrote, 'I know you are hiding in there.' Yeah, I am guilty of running away from my kids at times and hiding in the loo. Admit it, aren't you too?

There are real perils of encouraging kids to be communicative and honest, especially when it comes to someone like my daughter. I am continually entertained, harassed, challenged and embarrassed by her no-holds-barred comments and curiosity. I know these are qualities that I have nurtured but sometimes I wonder if my moral science lectures have created a Frankenstein's monster.

Take, for example, the time when I was getting chemotherapy. It was around my tenth or eleventh session. The exhausting treatment had begun to take a toll on my body and I would often feel weak. I had just had a bath and was heading to the dining room when I suddenly felt faint. My legs gave way, and I took support of a chair before I collapsed.

My boy came running to me in worry, as did my son who was nearly in tears. Little Miss Smarty Pants, all of five, was peering from behind them, unable to get to me. Loudly, she asked from her corner, 'Is she dead?' The question was asked out of curiosity and not concern. Instantly the temperature dropped in the room. I couldn't stop laughing; this fiery, inquisitive little girl of mine wouldn't even let me faint in peace.

Two years on, my daughter's curiosity and constant questions have only increased, frequently leaving me with no answers. She is currently in that phase when she'll interrupt the conversation if she hears a fancy word and ask for its meaning.

A friend of mine, who had moved to Canada, recently dropped in for a visit. She had lived in that great country for a mere five years but her accent was now more Canadian than Mr Trudeau himself.

We were having an animated conversation about real estate and the size of houses. She began to compare the two countries. The little one, who was playing with magna tiles next to us and stealing the makhanas meant for the guest, asked oh-so-innocently, 'What's masterburate?'

What the freaking hell! This was worse than my son and the 'f*ck, duck, suck' episode. Now it's true I have often sworn in front of the kids (sorry, sorry) but I am certain I have never used that word in front of her! And all those episodes of *My Little Pony* that she watches so avidly couldn't be teaching her such a word either.

As I was sputtering in shock, my friend asked her gently, rolling her 'r's, 'Wherrre did you hearrr that?' The little one pointed to her and said, 'You'! Was my Canada-bhakt friend some kind of secret pervert? But before I could question my daughter, she said, 'You only kept saying this while telling us about your big house.'

We were both baffled. Then I cracked the code. 'You mean master bed?' 'Maybe. But when she says it, it sounds like—' Before the little one could complete her sentence, my friend jumped to her own rescue and said (this time without rolling any 'r's), 'No no, it's master bed only, sweetheart!' Wow, the accent had just vanished. My daughter really was a genius!

Along with helping people return to their roots through her indiscretions, Smarty Pants has also protected me with her honesty even as she has sent me to embarrassment heaven. One day she was kissing her father on the cheek and asked why his face felt smooth and soft sometimes and prickly at other times? He told her the difference between being clean-shaven and having a stubble or a beard. 'So stubble hurts the most!' she exclaimed in triumph. He smiled at her observation.

But this smile wasn't to stay long. The next day an aunt and her husband came visiting. The little one hugged her and since Aunty was standing, she only managed to wrap herself around her legs.

Instantly she exclaimed, 'Aunty, you are poky even through the salwar; didn't you shave your stubble today like Daddy does?' They were mortified but I admit to feeling a secret pleasure, as this aunt of mine is rather pushy.

The conversation meandered from politics to cricket and finally stopped at everyone's favourite subject, Bollywood. They wanted to know all the gossip, but soon were giving us more than we knew. In fact, they were the insiders, their sources being gossip magazines, kitty sessions and Insta accounts.

The conversation moved from how star x had miraculously lost weight by following a special diet and star y's vampire facials to, of course, who was cheating and who was hooking up. They pried and poked and we nodded blankly.

My boy has very little patience for such talk and typically responds by saying, 'Were you under their bed and actually saw it?' But this time he couldn't use this line, as they were our relatives. Aunty went on to commiserate with me about the difficulty of seeing one's husband with so many girls. I completed her sentence in as sweet a voice as I could muster, 'You mean on screen, Aunty?'

She nodded but her beady eyes were on the lookout for any twinge of pain or hurt on my part. I controlled myself, wishing I could send my little bomb of a girl to hug her and remind her of the poky person she was.

Miss Smarty Pants must have sensed my annoyance. She jumped up to say, 'You know, Papa has many wives!' The aunt's eyes popped out. Now things were getting juicy. This was, after all, why she was visiting.

Sensing nuclear-level danger, I quickly butt in with a forced smile and asked my daughter what she meant. She said, 'Only husband and wives kiss na, Mama? So all the girls Papa is with in the movies must be his wives?' My boy and I chuckled and explained to her that wasn't the case and we all had a laugh.

Uncle and Aunty looked rather dissatisfied that their little jibe had resulted in so much joy. We were 1–1 now. As we wished them farewell, I wondered how fast the story of the many wives would travel, no doubt embellished at every turn. But the poky story has made it to my book. And that makes it 2–1. I guess my kids will always have their sinful mother's back!

In the meantime, our bathroom love saga continues. And I keep getting letters, instructions, caricatures, complaints, requests, all from under the door. A few days ago I retreated into the loo once again, this time to have a cry by myself. I was feeling overwhelmed and heartbroken by the constant bad news brought about by the pandemic and crying in front of the kids is still tough for me.

Anxieties have the irritating habit of playing hopscotch in your head. As I sat on my thinking pot feeling sad, I began to worry about other things. What kind of world are my children going to grow up in? Will my son pay attention to his lessons? What about my little girl and her antics? Had I done the right thing by encouraging her to express herself so vividly?

My reverie was broken when a paper came sliding in from under the door. The note said, 'It's okay, Mama, take your time, I promise I will make corona go away.' Reading her letter made me pin my hopes on the future generation rather than the current government. Maybe my moral science lectures hadn't gone to waste after all.

Acknowledgements

I am blessed to have such an amazing family. It's a wonder that after *The 12 Commandments of Being a Woman* and now this one they haven't disowned me. With each book I think I push my luck, hoping I don't run out of it! I am grateful in advance to my kids who will have no option but to roll their eyes and hopefully accept me once they reach an age when they can read my books. I also want to thank my publisher, Chiki, who is always guiding and pushing me and leaving no stone unturned to help me embarrass myself! I love her for that. Last but not the least, grateful to God for letting me experience being a woman.

A Note on the Author

Tahira Kashyap Khurrana is a writer and film-maker based in Mumbai. She is the author of four books, including the bestselling *The 12 Commandments of Being a Woman*, and has directed three acclaimed short films, *Pinni*, *Toffee* and *Quaranteen Crush*.

An Excerpt from
*The 12 Commandments of
Being a Woman*

Put doubts about yourself to rest
Believe in yourself – it's simply the best

As you may have guessed, I was a bit of an achiever in junior school. I stood first in all the elocution competitions and was always cast as the lead character in our school plays. And, of course, I earned a prefect badge for these glittering extracurricular activities.

Then, at age eleven came grade six and senior school. Senior school was a whole different beast. It was run differently, too. In junior school, there was a headmistress to whom the schoolteachers reported. Senior school – from sixth to twelfth grade – was run by the vice principal and the principal. I was sure I was going to rock it just like I had in junior school. But I was wrong.

I hadn't accounted for the politics between teachers. For if there are some pros of having your mother as a teacher (subsidized school fees being a big one), then there are lot of cons as well. Some teachers were nice to me because of my mother, but others weren't, especially those who didn't like her.

And somehow this co-curricular prefect wasn't chosen for any intra-school competitions, let alone interschool ones. I was denied all opportunities.

Initially I couldn't understand what was happening. My confidence began to drop, but my mother kept pushing me. 'You must prepare, you must participate,' she would tell me. I would argue with her, saying, 'I am not allowed to participate, let alone win!'

And so from sixth to ninth grade (as I struggled with not getting my periods and having no boobs), I added one more thing to my list of woes and another reason for my growing anger against my mother.

There came a time when I knew I wasn't going to be selected even before I stepped in front of the teachers for the try-outs. The chances of never making it were becoming stronger. It irritated me that my mother refused to get it. She would force me to stand with my prepared speech or poem. 'Keep trying, never give up' was all she said. I don't think she knew what it meant to be rejected all the time, every time.

Then came grade ten. The dreaded year we had been warned about since we were in grade two. Those momentous board exams, the marks of which would determine our future. Trust me, I haven't given a single interview where anyone has asked me about my board exams. Of course, what you become and how your character and skills develop do depend on the schools and colleges you attend, but this undue pressure isn't justified.

Like several others, the pressure of being in grade ten had haunted me since I was a kid. And now here I was, facing the precipice. No more wasting time. It was study, study, study. So when the school announced that there was to be an interschool competition in Delhi, no student came forward. Who do you think seized the opportunity? Yes, it was me.

Two of us were being sent by the school. I was participating in the English category and my partner was chosen for the Hindi segment. The day before we were to leave for Delhi, our vice principal called us to hear our prepared speeches. My partner killed it. She was really good and had learnt her piece by heart.

Me? Well . . . I was the same person who had been beaten down repeatedly for the last five years. I hadn't taken part in any of the school competitions, and here I was being sent not just to another school, but another city!

I gulped, my hands were sweaty, my knees buckled, and I stammered and fumbled my way through the piece. The vice principal nodded quietly, unable to give me even a word of encouragement, let alone the appreciation she gave my partner.

We went to Delhi in the Shatabdi train with our English teacher Ms Jyotsna. It's remarkable how a few moments with a positive person and a few words of motivation can light a fire in someone.

I saw my partner rehearse again and again despite knowing the speech by heart. Ms Jyotsna pushed me to do the same, and I could sense that she had faith in me. Perhaps all she wanted was for me not to forget my piece and fumble on stage, and I didn't want to prove her wrong either. And so I, too, rehearsed my piece for the three and a half hours of the train ride, without taking a minute's break.

My practice didn't end on the way to the hostel where we were put up, it didn't end during my dinner and it didn't end the next morning. It was twenty-four hours of constant rehearsal.

We arrived at Sawant Singh School, the venue of the competition. Thirty-three schools were participating. Two kids from each school. I was competing against sixty-six students! I had imagined fifteen students, twenty max. This was way out of my league. But I didn't stop rehearsing.

All the teams were really good, and had prepared well. They went on stage one after the other, while I waited in the wings for my turn. And then it was time. I stood on the dais. The auditorium was huge and filled with participants and teachers and other students.

I fixed my mic. I gulped, my hands were sweaty, my knees buckled, but I didn't fumble. It was as if I was where I had always wanted, and was meant, to be. The junior school co-curricular prefect resurfaced, and how!

I got so excited that I concluded the speech with a violent twirl of my hands and a quote by Napoleon, just like a little French revolutionary. Everyone loved it and clapped hard. I stepped down and sat next to Ms Jyotsna, who gave me a look of pride and a warm squeeze. And, honestly, that was enough for me.

Seeing my teacher's and the audience's response, I thought I would get a participation certificate. After what seemed like an endless wait, the results were announced. As the dignitaries called out the names of the kids who had won participation certificates, I waited to hear mine. But it wasn't announced. I felt really bad. Despite being rejected for five years, I still wasn't used to rejection.

I clapped along with the rest of the auditorium. Then they announced the name of the student who came third. I hoped against hope that I would make it, but my name was still not called out. Well, I wasn't really expecting it, I thought to myself, now feeling really deflated. The name of the student who had come second was announced. I continued clapping mechanically.

Then they announced the name of the student who had stood first among the sixty-six kids. Tahira Kashyap. I clapped. Ms Jyotnsa shook me. 'Whom are you clapping for? It's you, it's you!' I looked at her unbelievingly. I couldn't fathom what had happened.

In a daze, I didn't stop clapping even as I headed towards the stage to get my prize. People must have wondered what an overconfident girl I was, clapping for myself, but what they didn't realize was that these hands were used to clapping for others and they couldn't break the habit suddenly. I was on the stage. I had at most expected a certificate, but here I was with the biggest trophy.

A small embarrassing detail. After I won, I was numb for a while. And then it hit me. I went berserk with happiness. As we headed back to the hostel room, I couldn't contain my excitement and peed in my pants.

But that's what winning after five long years does to you. I am just so thankful to all those years of being rejected. The doused fire once reignited is nothing short of a blaze.

Everyone has their own love story Don't feel bad if yours isn't full of glory

At seventeen, my friends and I didn't know what falling in love really meant, though we were obsessed with the idea. We took male attention for granted – if you were an average-looking seventeen-year-old in Chandigarh, it was constant. It must be admitted, we weren't always kind to the boys. Every time I got the standard card and a chocolate from an admirer, I would accept the chocolate and shamelessly return the card.

The boys were ingenious. They hid their tokens of love in all sorts of places. I'd find a chocolate or a card or some stupid stuffed toy lying next to my bag or in my friend's scooter carrier or jammed under my car's wipers.

Thank god they spared the girls' washroom. Extracting chocolate from places like under the sink and behind the dustbin would have been gross, but not taking it would have been impossible. We were constantly hungry, you see. And treats, no matter who they were from, were always welcome.

My friends Divya and Prerna and I were preparing to become doctors. I mean, that was the intention. So we took tuitions to prepare for our PMT (premedical test).

Prerna and I went to the same tuition classes. In every class we shortlisted one boy as a prospective crush. In the physics class we both had a crush on a boy who was skinny but cute. It was a class of seventy, and we didn't know his name. Prerna and I were too careful (and snooty) to ask someone or to actually talk to any of the boys.

We were living at a time and in a place where inquiring after a boy would have cost us our reputation. We would have been labelled as easy. It's obnoxious, I know. It was the other way round when it came to us. The entire class knew our names. It's not that we were gorgeous, but that's how it was.

An Excerpt from *The 12 Commandments...*

In the film *Minority Report*, Tom Cruise just has to swipe his fingers in the air for information to pop up on a virtual screen. Ha! That was nothing compared to my batchmates who were a mix of Cruise and Arnold Schwarzenegger from *The Terminator*.

As soon as they locked sight of their target, not only would they know the girl's name, but her entire biodata would pop up in front of their retinas – house number, sector, phone number and also her status, whether it was single, committed or complicated.

This is one department in which I concede defeat to boys. Our skills were nowhere close to theirs. So we two Nancy Drews spent the entire year trying to figure out the name of that cute boy we liked with zero success.

Meanwhile, boys could dig out unknown details like the astrologer Maharishi Bhrigu, and know everything there was to know about the forefathers of the girl and the Google Maps location of her ancestral house before Partition, and nobody would judge them! I am convinced Google Maps was launched in the heads of the horny teenage boys of Chandigarh seven years before it actually made it to our phones in 2008! On the other hand, if a girl were to simply ask the name of a boy then she was easy or madly in love or wanted to get him beaten up!

Those Chandigarh boys

The gedi route was perhaps the best example of messed-up boy–girl relations in small-town India. What is gedi route? It was a unique Chandigarh phenomenon in which girls and boys chased each other mindlessly from sector 10 to sector 11 in their cars and scooters. The boys would be playing loud gabru music and pursuing the girls, and I would be lying if I said some girls didn't enjoy it.

Sector 10 was the closest market to my home and unfortunately lay at the heart of the gedi route. I had to cross it every time I drove to school and later college.

We didn't know what to say to our parents. We never discussed it with them because we didn't want to be dissuaded from leading normal teenage lives. For all you know, they could have banned us from driving around the city or taking tuitions in the evening. But, thankfully, none of the creepy teenage boys that followed us stuck around for long, except for a stalker I had at school who was finally scared away by my boy and his pals when we were in college.

Many Bollywood and Punjabi songs boast about this culture in their lyrics. It wasn't just the gedi route where we were followed. Boys, groups of boys, would be waiting for us after tuition class. At the end of every class we planned and mapped our exit and tried to fool the enemies. So when Narendra Modi came up with the surgical strikes in 2016, the planning wasn't new to us. We had been doing it ever since we hit puberty, some of us even before that.

We had two Kinetic Hondas and as per plan, we would go in two different directions and then meet at one common point. So much thinking went into this on a daily basis that had the same brain cells been used by the boys and us to understand the dynamics of chemical equations, at least some of us would have become doctors and justified spending our parents' money.

One winter evening, when the days are short and the nights set in pretty early, we began our usual exit operation after physics class. The boys followed and we tried to evade them. The race was interesting as we managed to leave two out of the four bikes behind. Before Hrithik Roshan knew how to do this in *Dhoom 2*, we had become experts. All that was left for us to learn was Ajay Devgn's balancing act on two vehicles.

So now two bikes were behind Divya and me, and god knows how many behind Prerna. Divya tried to make her way through the tiny streets and gullies, but they continued to follow us. We had run out of escape routes and were left with no choice but to enter my sector. Determined not to reveal my address to the boys, we stepped on to someone else's porch and pretended it was ours. Once we stopped the bikes, they usually left.

One day I would really like to know their side of the story. There must be a reason for behaving like jerks. However, that night one bike followed us straight to our fake house. Divya and I were hiding behind the gate, and we saw the rider take off his helmet. We were sweating even though it was ten degrees outside, clinging to each other. We looked at the man, and then at each other in confusion. It was Divya's father!

We felt relieved. Safe, but also violated. How can parents start following us? But looking at the positive side, we were happy that he would know we were doing nothing to provoke the boys to follow us. Yup, justification mode again. But then we started wondering if this was the first time Divya's father had followed us or if he had done it before. Had we ever given a wrong signal to the boys? By the end of it, we didn't know what to feel; we were being followed by both parties without our consent. Yet again, the female species in the small city was left confused.

Thank god times are changing, but Kabir Singh playing to the gallery and people appreciating it sends shivers down my spine. I found Shahid Kapoor very hot in the film, but what is glorified in it is something most of us dread in real life.

So the entire year went by with us calling our crush Coolio and leaving it at that. It was a really cheesy name, I know, but we found his gel-spiked hair and his cute specs, skinny frame and dimples really cool.

One day our test papers were being handed out. Prerna and I were all ears. This was our golden chance of discovering our boy's name. As soon as sir called out the name Abhishek, the paper was passed to Coolio.

Hmm . . . Abhishek. We made a mental note. We told Divya about this Abhishek boy and how cool he was on his Yamaha bike with the extra lights. Unable to contain her curiosity, Divya decided to bunk her tuition one evening to come to ours and take a look at him. She was the gutsiest of the three of us so perhaps she would even talk to him and open the door for us.

Divya arrived on her father's Vespa on the big day. We waved to her excitedly and she looked eager, too. Good-looking boys were a rarity and Coolio had been heavily built up in her head. Without switching off the engine, Divya looked in his direction and said, 'Yeh hai?'

We both nodded in unison.

With a look of disdain, she turned her scooter around and said, 'It's better I attend my class.'

'What?' Prerna and I cried out in surprise. 'She doesn't like him?' We dismissed it as lack of taste.

The year was coming to an end, and so was our physics class. Not a word was exchanged with Coolio, though I received around two dozen chocolates and cards from the other boys in the class.

One day my father declared that we had to go for a family dinner. 'Chandigarh is a small town. We didn't go for their house-warming party, so we all have to go for this dinner. He is specially organizing it for us.'

'Who is he?' I asked.

'He is a very renowned and respected astrologer.'

I quickly picked up the cordless phone. It had turned from white to grey and the numbers on the keys were faded – a sure sign that you have a teenager at home. I punched in Prerna's phone number, wishing I had a similar memory for equations.

'Tell your parents that if they allow you to attend this dinner with me then we will get to know our future and the money we are spending on classes and admission forms can be saved. Once you come, we'll tell my parents that we aren't in a mood to go, and we can chill the entire night.' We could hang out and make crank calls, one of the great joys of pre cell phone teenage life.

Prerna loved the idea. She took permission from her parents and came over. But our plan didn't go according to script. When we told my parents that we weren't in the mood to go, they insisted we come along. 'It's a family thing and we have also promised Prerna's parents that she will talk to astrologer uncle,' my mother said. Prerna looked at me in horror, but I was helpless.

The one saving grace in this mess was that our host had two kids. The elder one was apparently our age, so we'd have someone to talk with.

We reached their house and were seated in their living room. I looked around, taking in the room. There on the wall opposite me hung a big family portrait of the Raichands, with the mother and father sitting on chairs and the two sons standing behind them. One of the sons was Coolio!

I squealed, 'Prerna ... Coolio!' At that exact moment, Prerna saw him walk into the room to greet us, and squeaked, 'OMG, it's him!' I said, 'Where are you looking? He is ...' and there he was right in front of us.

This was a typical filmy Teja moment from *Andaz Apna Apna*. Prerna and I were grinning. We eagerly followed Coolio into another room (for the kids to hang out) and that's when we discovered this wasn't the Raichand family of *Kabhi Khushi Kabhie Gham* (same vibe though, trust me), these were the D'Souzas. On the wall of this room was another picture of the four of them, this time with the mom in a frock, the father wearing suspenders and the sons sporting bow ties.

Of course, they weren't the D'Souzas or the Raichands. They were the Khurranas. And he wasn't Abhishek, he was ... well, why would you be interested. He was just a boy who was melting our hearts because after my father sang (he is a trained classical singer), this boy started crooning 'Bade acche lagte hain', which had Prerna and me swooning. That one dinner cost our parents years of crazy phone bills and, a decade later, marriage banquet hall charges.

Within a few months of that dinner, I was seeing my boy. The attraction between us was high. We mostly had movie dates at a single-screen theatre called Nirman in sector 32. That year we watched *Aśoka* fourteen times. Kareena Kapoor's 'San sana na na nan' rang in our ears as we clung to each other.

The movie that beat *Aśoka*'s record for us was *Lajja*, which we watched nineteen times. We knew the storyline of *Aśoka*, as my boy was a big SRK fan, and we watched it properly at least once. But when it comes to *Lajja* I draw a blank, as we spent all those hours ... well, discussing chemistry equations.

An Excerpt from *The 12 Commandments...*

It took us six months to get to first base. But it stopped there, despite my boy's every attempt to take us to second base. I really did test his patience.

I was nineteen and still not confident about my breasts. Even though they were decent-sized, watching *Baywatch* had set standards that I could only dream of. By now some clever company, seeing the distress of women, had brought padded bras to India.

I bought mine from a humble store in sector 35 that Divya and Prerna had introduced me to. It was called Fancy Store, but it was not very fancy as they had limited styles and sizes and we invariably needed to force our assets into the bras that came closest to our size.

Emboldened by my bra, we did go to second base, but it was much harder than I had imagined, because we never had a place to ourselves. There was a disastrous trip to a hill station, and one scary time when he came home and my father nearly caught us in the act.

With not many options left for two horny teenagers, we gave in to the inevitable. We made our friend drive my boyfriend's silver Santro Xing around town while we had a great time in the back seat.

Of course, we made sure he had turned the rear-view mirror away from us and a couple of times we noticed him turning up the volume of the music, too. 'Rhythm divine' and 'Hero' by Enrique Iglesias would make me swoon and the car would swerve just on cue. Yet, despite our chemistry and us getting closer, I never stopped dreaming of getting triple D cups.

We were having a gala time. Then something happened that changed everything. Now my boy and I were united by our mutual attraction. But we had a lot else in common as well, especially our love for theatre and public speaking.

This often resulted in us being pitted against each other at college competitions. He represented DAV College, sector 10, and I was at GGDSD College, sector 32. So in a way we were lovers who were often rivals.

We were both gearing up for the annual youth festival where we were acting in our respective college's plays. Rehearsals took hours every day and we weren't able to see much of each other.

The big day came. The competition was being held at Khalsa College, sector 26. The college building was buzzing with the energy of all the teams getting ready.

An Excerpt from *The 12 Commandments...*

The classrooms had been turned into make-up rooms.

We hadn't seen each other for a while. Being ultra-competitive, we hadn't even discussed the plots of our plays with each other. And today we would be seeing each other on stage.

Now you have to imagine this in slow motion. We are both in the wings of the stage. My performance is right before his. We look at each other. I am dressed up as a transsexual and he as a bald man.

His play is about bald guys, so backstage was bobbing with bald heads. Beefy baldies, thin baldies, tall baldies, short baldies, baldies with specs, braces and pimples. And among this sea of bald boys, there is a flat-headed one with a skinny body, bushy brows and a dimple which has my heart. I cheered madly from the side as they began their performance.

My look was as dramatic as my boy's. I was wearing a garish glittery suit that could blind anyone. At five feet, eight and a half inches, I really suited the part, and don't think I required much make-up. All those years of 'Oh, you look just like your father' were coming to my aid that day. On stage I spoke in a Bachchan-type heavy bass voice, and I could see my boy smiling in the wings.

As we cheered each other on, our pupils dilated, we

got goosebumps and our knees went weak. That day, my friends, we fell in love with each other. True and weird love.

I have heard many unusual love stories about the moment a couple fell in love. None have come close to being this odd. I had to become a transsexual and he had to be bald for us to really fall for each other.

His team won and ours came third. Still light-headed from the feeling of love, we didn't cool our hormones off in the theatre, but went to the lake instead where he, as always, sang a song for me. 'Bade acche lagte hain . . . yeh nadiya'. My glittery suit sparkled in the water as did his shiny head in the winter sun.

juggernaut

THE APP
FOR INDIAN
READERS

Fresh, original books tailored for mobile and for India. Starting at ₹10.

juggernaut.in

1

CRAFTED FOR MOBILE READING

Thought you would never read a book on mobile? Let us prove you wrong.

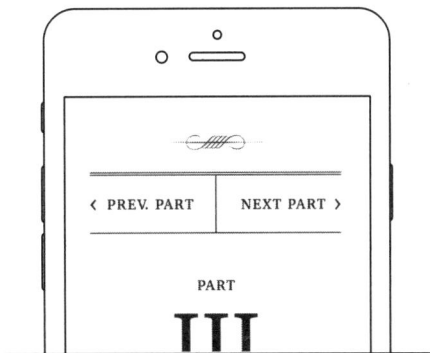

PREV. PART | NEXT PART

PART

III

Beautiful Typography

The quality of print transferred
to your mobile. Forget ugly PDFs.

spleen and regulating the circulation.
Whenever I find myself growing grim
about the mouth; whenever it is a
damp, drizzly November in my soul;
whenever I find myself involuntarily
pausing before coffin warehouses, and

T− | T+

Aa | Aa | Aa | Aa

Customizable Reading

Read in the font size, spacing
and background of your liking.

AN EXTENSIVE LIBRARY

Including fresh, new, original Juggernaut books from the likes of Sunny Leone, Praveen Swami, Husain Haqqani, Umera Ahmed, Rujuta Diwekar and lots more. Plus, books from partner publishers and loads of free classics. Whichever genre you like, there's a book waiting for you.

CRUCIBLES OF SIN
HITESHA

Can a Geek ever find Love?
Finding Juliet
Toffee

Mary Shelley
Frankenstein

A FAROOQ RESHI INVESTIGATION
COLD FLAKE
PRAVEEN SWAMI

How to Heal Your Broken Heart
Psychiatrist's Guide To Heartbreak
DR SHYAM BHAT

MOIN and THE MONSTER
BY ANUSHKA RAVISHANKAR

stories of women from the danglands
Mafia Queens of Mumbai
S. Hussain Zaidi
with Jane Borges
Foreword by Vishal Bhardwaj

Pakistan's Queen of Romance
UMERA AHMED
Nowhere Girl
A Story of Love & Forgiveness

THE BEHEADING
This Is How He Will Bless Her
ABHEEK BARUA

THE Peshwa
The Lion and the Stallion

THE INVISIBLE WOMAN
A SUSPENSE MURDER MYSTERY THAT WILL MAKE YOU EXCLAIM THE END
SAURBH KATYAL

ANGRY BIRDS FANS READ THE BOOK!
ANGRY BIRDS TOONS
TOONS TALES

ARCHANA SABOO
ADIKOOL in #AfricanAdventures

i am not a bimbette
Tarana Khan

She hates me. He loves me not but...
DON'T FALL IN LOVE
Vandana Shankar

KHUSHWANT SINGH
WE INDIANS

3

DON'T JUST READ; INTERACT

We're changing the reading experience from passive to active.

Ask authors questions

Get all your answers from the horse's mouth.
Juggernaut authors actually reply to every
question they can.

Rate and review

Let everyone know of your favourite reads or
critique the finer points of a book – you will be
heard in a community of like-minded readers.

Gift books to friends

For a book-lover, there's no nicer gift than
a book personally picked. You can even
do it anonymously if you like.

Enjoy new book formats

Discover serials released in parts over
time, picture books including comics,
and story-bundles at discounted rates.
And coming soon, audiobooks.

juggernaut.in

4

LOWEST PRICES & ONE-TAP BUYING

Books start at ₹10 with regular discounts and free previews.

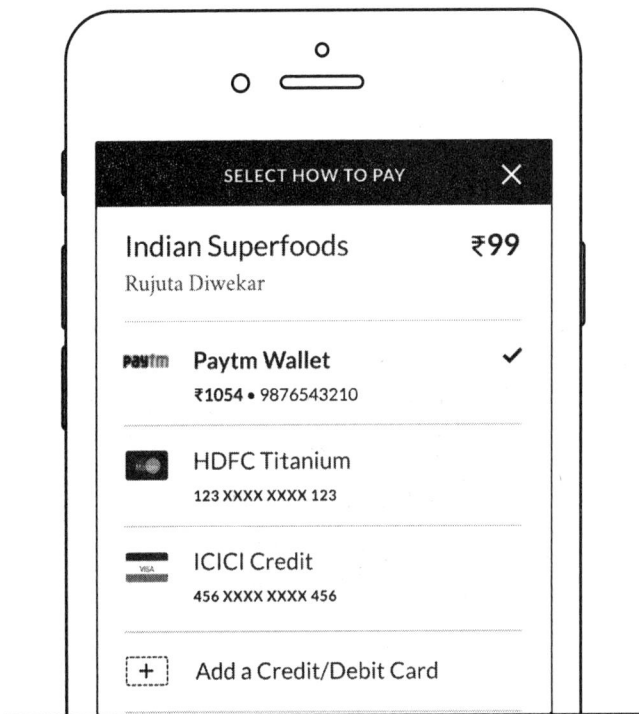

SELECT HOW TO PAY

Indian Superfoods ₹99
Rujuta Diwekar

Paytm Wallet ✓
₹1054 • 9876543210

HDFC Titanium
123 XXXX XXXX 123

ICICI Credit
456 XXXX XXXX 456

+ Add a Credit/Debit Card

Paytm Wallet, Cards & Apple Payments

On Android, just add a Paytm Wallet once and buy any book with one tap. On iOS, pay with one tap with your iTunes-linked debit/credit card.

To download the app scan the QR Code
with a QR scanner app

For our complete catalogue, visit www.juggernaut.in
To submit your book, send a synopsis and two
sample chapters to books@juggernaut.in
For all other queries, write to contact@juggernaut.in